# The History of Naming Cows

# The History
## of
## Naming Cows

Mitch Spray

*To Rachel
and friendship*

*[signature]*

Hagios Press
Box 33024 Cathedral PO
Regina SK   S4T 7X2
www.hagiospress.com

Copyright © 2012 Mitch Spray

All rights reserved. No part of this publication may be reproduced, stored in a retrieval system, or transmitted in any form or by any means without the prior written permission of the publisher or by licensed agreement with Access: The Canadian Copyright Licensing Agency. Exceptions will be made in the case of a reviewer, who may quote brief passages in a review to print in a magazine or newspaper, broadcast on radio or television, or post on the Internet.

**Library and Archives Canada Cataloguing in Publication**

Spray, Mitch

   The history of naming cows / Mitch Spray.

(Strike fire new authors series)

Poems.

ISBN 978-1-926710-15-0

   I. Title.  II. Series: Strike fire new authors series

PS8637.P73H58 2012     C811›.6     C2012-901525-3

Edited by Allan Safarik.
Designed and typeset by Donald Ward.
Cover art: "Ophelia II," sculpture by Joe Fafard.
Artwork photographed by Brent Komonosky.
Cover design by Tania Wolk, Go Giraffe Go Inc.
Set in Minion Pro.
Printed and bound in Canada.

The publishers gratefully acknowledge the assistance of the Saskatchewan Arts Board and The Canada Council for the Arts in the production of this book.

*To my parents, Brian and Karen,
for their support*

# Contents

**Dreaming Home**

My Hills   10
Between Trees   11
The Dog's Bear   12
Mom's Gardens   13
Austin Forty   15
Sons   16
Dreaming Home   17
Our Barn   18
Making Bread   19
Canning   20
She Rears Back and Fires   21
Time with Grandpa   23
*Old Puss*   25
Dog Named *Stupid*   26
Hunting, 1973   27
Horseshoes   28
Old Danger   29
The Snow Fort   30
Pond Hockey Triptych   31

**Animal Husbandry**

Handling Cows   34
Small Trees   35
Damn Black Cow   36
The Bull's Skurr   37
Manure Pile Loving   38
Bull Hide   39
Leaves of Alfalfa   40
Two Halves   41
The History of Naming Cows   43
*Salt*   45

From the Tractor Seat  46
The Penicillin Arrow  47
Scours  50
Genetic Udder Conformity  52
Out Shoveling  53
Farm Grown  54
Chaff  56
Snow Steam Holes  59
In the Dead of Winter  60
Condensation Ice  62
Four Inches of Tongue  63
At the Vet's  65
*Liz*  67

**New Land**

The Versatile Eight Hundred  70
Returning to the City  72
Bush Pasture and an Old House  73
New Land  76
Thirty-five Acres in Retrospect  77
Baling  80
One Beer  81
The Baler  82
Salvaged  83
Grandpa Stooking  87
Chainsaw Memories  88
A Christmas Story  90
The Need for Scotch  91
Reverie  93

# Dreaming Home

**My Hills**

My childhood hills are green, strewn with rocks.
The small sloughs green and soft, brighter than the dry hills.

Standing at the dugout, careful not to fall in
we threw sticks and stones, stared at underwater weeds
on the edge of the springtime slough rubber boot deep.

Behind the barn under two towering spruce my brothers
and I gathered the burnt ends of bulldozing rows.
Stacked them between the tree trunks. Ants
continued our defence against the milk cow's nosiness.

The anthill grew three feet inside the fence.
We couldn't resist stabbing in sticks, and rubber boots,
throwing stones. At two Brett wore ants around his neck
screaming. The anthill now obliterated under the hay yard.

The farm marches on, across these hills.
Bales piled three high every fall, fifteen feet high,
twenty-thousand cubed feet of feed. Hay, straw,
and manure cover my pristine hills.

I attach old memories to this new landscape,
understand corrals constructed to trick cows.
Manure pushed into piles. I appreciate the glow
of new planks, the warp of aging wind fence.

**Between Trees**

Laughing, three brothers
run between pasture trees
chase a garter snake
long as my arm.
Mouth open shouting,
I taste a spiderweb
stretched between tree branches.

I paw my face, ears.
Snake forgotten,
tadpoles wait to be discovered
in the dugout and slough
on the Little Pasture's edge.

**The Dog's Bear**

Dogs barking
non stop at six a.m.

Dad wakes, lies listening to them,
finally he rises, gets dressed,

jeans, shirt open,
barefoot into rubber boots.

He follows their cacophony to the spruce
just off the farmyard garden.

The dogs have a yearling bear wrapped
around a tree trunk. Dad shakes his head,
strolls back to the house, loads three shells
into the 30-30 Winchester carbine.

With one shot the bear drops,
wedged into the V of the tree trunks.
Stuck, the bear stunk all summer.

**Mom's Gardens**

1.

In my mother's garden,
weeds always out of control
until finally, one year, her guilt
gazing upon the shameful garden
got the better of us. Weeds rivaling corn,
twice as tall as potato plants,
pink pig weed, hiding in the shade, filled
five gallon pails, pail after pail
of purple blossomed thistle tossed to
three pigs, slobbering, chomping
through the pails of mom's guilt.

2.

Lilacs line the turnaround loop
grown bushy with neglect
round and soft dust bunnies

last year's grass
golden through the branches
between dusty green leaves

Dad fills a baby food jar
with purple sprigs
scents the dining room table.

3.

In the city, my wife
on her knees weeds
a small flowerbed beneath
the front yard weeping birch.

I remember my mother. Blue knee pads,
weeding the flower bed she dreamed
at the end of the house
where the doghouses now sit.
The roses I transplanted
choking on grass and dogs.

I smile,
blow a bemused breath
at our suburban postage stamp.

**Austin Forty**

Ten feet off the farmyard where we played
football, soccer, five hundred,
ran ourselves skinny,
the ancient truck sits dead
the colour of moldy bread,
lead paint, the deep green of fish backs.
It sits surrounded by black poplars, wild raspberries.
The chrome bumper winks brightly through pitted rust.

A lone chrome wiper arm embraces emptiness.
Wood seat mounts are empty and grey.
The glove box full of old leaves
chrome boxed white gauges.

Both lament the empty steering column
and four feet of pipe that became
Dad's sprinkler stand
a sprinkler we couldn't jump.

Half hidden, the rear frame's suspension pots
are full of leaf mold. The shaded rock pile
pushes the door toward the chrome scripted
*Austin of England,* someone's imported pride.

A squirrel darts into the empty wheel well,
hides behind the broken grill,
crest in the centre, ruby diagonal
on periwinkle, two silver lions
proclaim *Austin 40.*

Lichen encrusted rocks, steps
for climbing the short nosed hood
roof popping under lifted feet.
A single orange coated wire
holds a rusted headlamp.

**Sons**

*His body flexed with work and frost[1]*

Oblivious, his sons pursue
the same broken body.

They feel his strength in their muscles.
Shovel grain, carry calves,
cut wood, swing axes and sledgehammers.

Pulling wrenches they revel in flexing muscles.
His gift to them. Blind to the regret
behind his sun beaten face.
His sapped strength distilled in sons.

---

1   From Sheri Benning's "Descent From the Cross" in *Thin Moon Psalm*

**Dreaming Home**

I wander over broken stones
piled here by my father's hands,
remember him picking rocks
tall above my awe.

I feel them roll under my feet,
know the sweat, the effort
muscles bulging, the stone's
weight pulling at my hands.
Sweat, dust on my face.

I love washing the dirt away
in the bathroom off the kitchen,
smelling the roast and its gravy
with potatoes and carrots,
tea in the pot, in my cup.
Mom sits waiting for us.

Eating with appetite,
we listen to the radio's country music.

**Our Barn**

— *I'm gonna paint the barn*
— *What colour*
— *Purple*
— *You can't paint a barn purple*
— *Wanna bet*

barn paint sale
pails of white tinted purple
purple as they could make it

                                  inside
                an orange tom cat
tossed from a laughing child's hands
         lands on his feet
frantically climbs rough spruce studs

                                  outside
           young boys on a silver tractor
      chase a fenceless cow,
hit the barn, drive the tractor's bale tines,
two round holes into lilac plywood,
purple as they could make it.

**Making Bread**

The teal t-shirt, tight
across her breasts,
her bra straps stand out.
Her shoulders stir the giant bread bowl,
stainless steel on the counter.
The white flour pail sits
on her kitchen chair.

From below, my five-year-old eyes
watch her shoulders work.
I lose count of cups
of flour. Lard, chicken or pork,
out of resealed Cheez Whiz jars.

Hot water and yeast. All kneaded by hand,
turned and punched,
kneaded by my five-foot-four mother.

A mound of dough becomes twenty-four loaves,
and a pan of cinnamon buns with raisons.

Dough rolled out, buttered,
brown sugar and cinnamon
scattered. Raisons applied thick.
All rolled into a white sticky log.

The tube choked with a thread,
cut into thirteen buns,
carefully lifted, placed
into the scarred cake pan.
Rising covered with an old towel,
peaking through the scraggly square hole.

**Canning**

standing on a chair
hands on the counter
I watch her shucking
peach skins in August's heat

dipped in boiling water
blanched peach hides
slide free like the scalded beets
she skinned days before.

Her favourite paring knife
follows the peach's cleavage
frees the nut from the centre.

She fills jars, tops them
with sugar water

the canner bubbling
jars sterilizing
steam rises

sweat runs down her side.

## She Rears Back and Fires

I.

five years old,
the sister of three older brothers,
playing in the farmyard

throwing a ball
awkwardly underhand
running to retrieve it

the old red Ford slides down the driveway,
returning from the field, it leans forward,
the brake crushed as he yells

> DON'T THROW LIKE A GIRL

it's supper time but Dad spends half an hour
patiently teaching his girl to throw overhand

> *As hard as you can now, that's it.*

Mom meets him at the door

> *You know,*
> *that's your daughter*
> *you just told not to throw like a girl*

grinning, he washes the dirt from his hands

II.

the last week of September

Anita doesn't recognize the frozen seed rule

Shane running, mocks her
she picks up a discarded runty potato

rears back and fires,
smokes him in the temple
with that hard little red potato

his feet fly up into the air
he lies on the ground,
thrashing, swearing
under the apple tree

Brett and I laughing,
barely contain his anger

**Time with Grandpa**

I.

Thanksgiving, a silver pie plate
scattered pumpkin pie crumbs.
Grandpa won't say a word,
but we all see his eyes stray
an orange bowl of whipped cream.
a glint in his eye,
an impish smile dips
the spoon into the rich froth.

II.

At a wedding dance

*See the one in red over there?*
*She left her no good husband three weeks ago.*
*She'll be ready and willin' for ya.*
*twenty-three, she ain't much older than you.*

*Yeah okay    sure Grandpa.*

III.

On his son-in-law's farm
retirement occupied with headlands

and desire, crops and
summers of watching

abandoned scrap piles grow over
with quack grass and rose bushes.
Ankle twisting treachery old man risked
to find a possible piece of rebar,
an old hitch pin or pry bar, a box iron
bale trailer crossbeam, a drive shaft or pulley.

With his rusted cant hook, the day after he died, I manhandle
poplar logs onto the scrap pile scavenged sawmill
Grandpa designed.

*Old Puss*

I was seven
the day I found *Old Puss*
the cat that had five kittens
every year like clockwork.
I found her, the calico cat,
in the willow thicket under the spruce
her body flattened by time,
fur matted with rot. I flipped her over
with the toe of my running shoe,
a large black bug skittered from beneath her.
I never loved a cat again
not like I loved *Old Puss*
the cat older than me
until the day I was seven

She's the only cat I remember
anyone buying medicine for

I imagine because someone
ran up from the barn
voice high and pleading

*Mommy, Mommy*
*Old Puss is sick. She's sneezing*
*and her eyes are yucky*

**Dog Named *Stupid***

a curious little puppy,
out of Barry's dog *Old Pup*
too smart for his own good,
always getting into fixes
he couldn't get out of

course me and Barry named him *Stupid*

gave him to our brother-in-law
tried to change that dog's name
you could yell anything but

until he heard *Stupid* nothin' doin',
when he did he'd come a waggin'

sure gave that salesman a shock
when Jackie yelled

*Shuddup Stupid*
at the yappy bastard

Old Wilf sure got it too
when Vera saw what a dog
he turned out to be

*you know those boys better*
*than to turn down a dog*
*'cause of its name*

**Hunting, 1973**

In the truck guns loaded
the ranger appears over the hill

*unload   quick*
all three lever actions
click   clack
shells fly

Bang!

*What the Hell!*

Eyes swing to Barry
a hole in his boot
through the floor boards

*It's okay, I'm fine.*

Three days later
everyone's ready for bed
except Barry
he's downstairs
dressing his little toe.
shot the end clean off
never said a word.
waited till night every night
waited to dress it.

Thought we'd never know.

**Horseshoes**

Grandma is telling tales of Dad's childhood.
He, of course, refuses her version
of the truth with a lopsided grin.

> *Oh she's going senile,*
> *doesn't remember it*
> *the way it happened.*

He pauses, either to recall,
or cast himself in a better light.

> *Me and Barry were playing horseshoes.*
> *Marge, Mom's favourite, stood*
> *in front of the peg so she could play.*
> *I threw the horseshoe to miss.*
> *Thinking I meant to hit her*
> *Barry pushed her right into its path,*
> *Square in the head. I would'a missed.*
> *We hid the rest of the day.*
> *caught hell at supper.*

Grandma's response when I tell her this "truth."

> *All I know is your Dad threw the horseshoe*
> *and Marge had a bloody egg*
> *sized lump on her head.*

**Old Danger**

One brake
on the damn thing

Two-toned black
and silver 1980 F-150

Top of the line
twenty years before

Little brother driving
back roads at fifteen

Younger sister driving
fields at twelve

She hit fence posts
He hit a deer

In a truck older than both

**The Snow Fort**

each night after chores
we'd start snowballs rolling
me in my orange striped toque
my phony fur jacket
with safety pinned zipper

two brothers
we'd roll until
our feet slipped
and the snowball stalled

Dad would take it
roll it as big as he could
built a u-shaped fort
lifted our half snowballs
topped the snow fort, tall as him
cleared a half acre of snow

in the photograph his hair is bushy black
wings out the bottom of his navy blue toque

a giant, bearded, with smiling eyes
he hugs us to his cold coat
hot breath against our ears
in the castle he built
under the yard light

**Pond Hockey Triptych**

November
we stay off the dugout
the first few days
wait to be sure of ice
after three weeks
of twenty below
shinny is avoiding
slough grass and wind
roughened raspy spots
firewood or winter boots
goalposts

December
dugout ice
littered with cracks
four inch holes
ax shaped
shreeved by skates
I skate alone
hear the ice groan
watch the centre drop
settle, bind
rest again on water beneath
the ice silent
beneath my skates

January
the dugout's white expanse
stares at me
demands why
grey ice isn't exposed
my skates shattering
the moonlight gleam

# Animal Husbandry

**Handling Cows**

hundreds shuffle, packed tight
in the smallest corral

thrice a year treated and sorted
they circle, a slow maelstrom.
hooves and wet noses, snorting,
bawling, vaccinated and branded

squeezing cows up the chute,
to waiting needles, panels
pulled behind them. We strike
them about the ribs and head
turn them back toward vaccinations

a few blink at noses struck,
ignore rubber canes, waving arms,
shut out pain

these blinking ones
get gentle pressure

patience and hope the only option

separated into purebreds and crosses,
cow calf pairs, or cows weaned from calves

**Small Trees**

a dry summer of too many cows
pasture chewed dust

nothing but space between trees
underbrush ate forest

adventures could be had
a life imagined lying on my back

a twig beneath my shoulder blade
staring into leaves the sun

high above my eyebrows
one cow has begun pushing

leaning over small trees
the herd eats leaves

**Damn Black Cow**

the old black bitch
didn't come home that night
Barry went looking
found her in a little hollow
sleeping
kicked that old bitch
hard as he could

that bear took off one way
and Barry the other
never could guess
who was scareder
but we could smell it

**The Bull's Skurr**

his Charolais forehead blood smeared
fighting the neighbour's Hereford
he knocked off a skurr
        a knobby pseudo horn
              a grey rock
              a petrified turd
              on the side of his head
bled all over himself

the low frequency bullish trumpeting,
deep bellaring, resonates in my chest.
He's ferocious in his new battle face
no longer the friendly giant

tied to a corral post he jumps
the fence, nearly hangs himself
luckily he was tied long, except
tied short, he never could have done it

**Manure Pile Loving**

love-making not so gentle
twenty-two hundred pounds
of four-year-old Charolais

climbs aboard the eight-hundred-pound heifer

her downhill footing unsure in the rotted manure pile

she collapses to her knees
unseats him into the rich loam
his white hide soiled

on solid ground he remounts

**Bull Hide**

the sharp barb on his belly scratches so good

old iron willow pickets lean
drunkenly, sway with his dancer's

hip driven belly scratch
heaving his weight into the single
strand, brittle brown wire

grey posts, rotten teeth,
moss footed, lichen crowned,

lift off their stumps
expose their dark brown rot

silver splices hold together rust
wire leaves brown lines on his belly

he ambles away sated

**Leaves of Alfalfa**

Under the barn's mangers musty grey alfalfa
leaves escape the cow tongue's four stomachs.

The barn's mosaic floor of straw
and shit crunches dryly —
frozen, compacted —
breaks like particle board.

Summer's alfalfa leaves
wind-whispering,
green and alive,

brown almond skin,
the brittle brown of old paper,
the powder of moth wings.

Dusky white moths of cabbage,
cauliflower, and lettuce rows,
moths of alfalfa fields nearly ready,
just days from full bloom. Cut —
dried — rolled and tied.
sun-dried fragrant bales, spun and stacked,

grappled, dropped, twines cut.
Alfalfa fed into empty metal feeders,
benign cages, empty of feral lions
or tigers, all that remain are leaves, dry
and dusty beyond cow tongues reach
green on the snow.

**Two Halves**

I remember the rope. The grey lariat
wrapped around the silver grey
of the white poplar trunk.

The white faced calf, grown
into the white faced steer.

Grandpa tied the calf I named
to the strong poplar outside the barn door

I remember the knot, the grey frayed end
*Billy's* white face in the sights
of the .22 in my father's hands.
Shooed away I hid behind Mom's leg,
stared at the knot.

The shot's shock
made me jump and *Billy* drop.
A twist of the knife in Grandpa's hand
opened *Billy's* neck.

Then he hung
tied to tractor tines,
bloody face bent, pressed
to the ground. Rope ran
through the knees' knife hole
Mother, Father, Grandpa skinned him
while Grandma sharpened dull knives on stone.

Soon it was time to bag the asshole,
Grandpa tied it off with pink twine. Careful

not to puncture the bowels, Dad's two fingers
forced space for the knife. Billy's diaphragm opened
the guts spun out, heart, liver
land topside.
                Carcass swaying,
five hundred pounds jerked by the meat saw.

I stared at the two halves of beef while
Dad and Grandpa argued about quartering
between the third or fourth rib.

**The History of Naming Cows**

*Kick in the Head*,
a calf kicked by a horse.
She walked in circles,
slowly tightening circles
'til she fell over, legs going.
A good-looking heifer; outgrew it
kept her for years. Old *Kick in the Head*
was a damned good cow.

*Lucky*,
born Friday, December 13, 1987.
Dad named her *Lucky*, black skin
and white hair. I watch her black nose dip,
rise wet from the yellow and red *Richie*™ watering bowl.
Her hips jut out behind picket fence ribs,
the pink udder hangs black tips. A bony heifer
became a bony cow, but in 'eighty-eight
Dad was desperate for heifers, this ugliest piece
of cow flesh stayed around. *Lucky*
to be alive, kept her 'til she was fourteen.
The Holstein in her raised dandy calves.

*Captain Floppy*, Gelbveih bull his pedigree reads
*Captain Call of the Lonesome Dove Ranch.*
Twenty-five-hundred bucks,
woulda' been four grand but he has a floppy ear,
tag hit a nerve. He can't lift
his left ear above half mast.
looks good coming out
of the sales ring. They poured
the feed to him. Two years later, his hair
is rough and shaggy. He shows every rib in the pasture.

*Off*. You can't tell anyone to fuck *Off*
at our place. She's in the pasture.

*Cupid*, Brett's first purebred calf
born February 14, '05 horned,
nobody'd buy him for breeding.
Good looking animal even without
heavy rations. Brett thought we'd eat him
after one breeding season but Dad
uses him again and again. At three
he shames the sale ring bull,
Makes *Captain* look gaunt.

*Salt*

Sunny or rain soaked,
I ran a mile the whole summer
to walk amongst the cows,
count their number to forty-three.

Twice a day I fed *Salt*,
the bottle-fed calf
taken from his mother
short milk for twins.

*Salt,* the twin Dad sold us
so we would feed it, never bunted
as bottle-fed calves usually do.

*Salt*, the white twin to red *Pepper*.

He grew large, strong, a six
hundred pound steer, easily
petted, fawned over by boys,

unafraid, we let our six-
year-old sister crawl under his belly.

We traded him to Dad
for the yearling heifer named *Storm*
he was sold and we had profit put off
into the cycle of calving and selling.

## From the Tractor Seat

Sun in my eyes, the field unfurls itself,
swaths bake between tractor tires.

Helios — the Greek god — shines down,

bestows heat in a rain-ravaged year
but cloud shadows dance across the fields.

The tractor seat yearns for the sun
to protect drying alfalfa from rain
blackened stalks, mushy leaf mold.

Spring floods, summer soakers fill sloughs
not yet cut, baled. A fall of frost and rain,

pulling wrenches I'm cold to the bone.
Flexing freezing fingers, I understand sun worship,
sacrifices to angry vengeful gods.

Bring on the virgin bull, muscle heavy, well fed
the god's bull, babied, fed by my hand.

I'll take the knife, slit its throat.
You catch the blood for the damn greedy god.

*Mitch Spray*

## The Penicillin Arrow

I.

I drive the white truck
chasing a black cow

Brett hangs, left handed
bow and arrow out the window
to treat her udder infection

bouncing across mole hills
we chase the Welsh Black's loping
her bag swinging wildly

the syringe/arrow released
bounces off her hip bone
the needle hooks into her ear
air pressure pushes penicillin

II.

a calf hops on three legs
Dad follows while I circle
attempt to distract the calf

he stops and stares at me
I meet his eye

the crossbow snaps
the penicillin arrow hits his tail bone

lacking penetration it drops unspent
we take another ten minute walk
around a limping calf

III.

white hair thin and patchy
across her Charolais hip bone
the skinny jutting bones of illness
pink hip skin flakes in the cold
her breath is raspy, either pneumonia
or something caught in her throat

I crossbow arm myself
the pink projectile launched
hits pumps falls away spent

leaves a pink drop of penicillin on her thigh

**Scours**

Brett's calf *Red Bull* refuses to die.
Morning medicine stomach tubed
through the stiff plastic pipe,
carefully inserted, held back, until
the calf swallows, avoids drowning.
Electrolytes fortified with a raw egg
or molasses, Pepto Bismol and peroxide
propelled down his throat by a syringe,
ginger and brown sugar in warm water,
home remedies, anything
we've ever heard treats scours.

Of course there's the mother to deal with,
snorting, charging the box stall boards
pulling up short pawing. Damn dumb cow
trying to intimidate us, each pull of her hoof
kicks *Red Bull* in the head
we leave her, *She'll calm down,* we hope.

That afternoon a busted gate,
broken boards. The cow
two stalls from the calf,
bawling for him

the next day Brett's fiancée shouts
across the barnyard, *The cow's out.*

I run, look, she's knocked down the metal panel
we're using for a gate. Knocked it onto *Red Bull.*
She stands over him, proud of herself.
The metal panel pressed into his flesh.

Going back to the city I'm optimistic,
convinced that this calf will live,
he's started to hold his head up.
In a week he'll be sleek and running,
red against golden oat straw,
blinding snow.

But I know he might die,
be skinned, his hide
draped over the abandoned calf *Crazy,*
the skin's scent convincing the grieving mother
this orphan is hers.
No more milk replacer,
udders always available,
no twice-a-day, two litre
rubber nipple feedings
powdered milk,
lumps whisked out,
as smooth as we can get it.

Later that week I call home, ask,

> *Did Red Bull survive?*

Nope.

> *Too bad.*
> *So did ya get Crazy onto the cow?*

No, the shit nuts cow broke the gate again.

**Genetic Udder Conformity**

as the country boy
in a poets' gathering
I'm an instant expert.
from my mouth I hear
a sales ring phrase
*Genetic Udder Conformity*

months later looking at cattle with Dad
*She's got a shitty bag,* but
with a tilt of his head,
*We'll keep her one more year*

**Out Shoveling**

Shoveling barley, lungs ache, neck itches.
I don't dare quit. Dad is going strong.
I pause, breathe deep, cough.
      The auger rattles,
the gaping maw demands grain.

Finally done,
we climb awkwardly
out the bin's small door.
I hook my unzipped ducky parka
on a nail, stumble out the door.
Our eyes catch, he's breathing hard,
one-armed leaning against the plywood bin.

> *Why the hell didn't you stop for a break?*
> *I coulda' used one.*
>
> *I wasn't stopping before you, Old Man.*
> *Me neither, couldn't let you outwork me.*

Hork, spit black grain dust,
we cough at the catch of a deep breath,
move to the next wood bin.

**Farm Grown**

I.

Two five-gallon pails of chop,
white cows, noses in buckets,
twelve hundred pounds of curiosity
pull at my teenaged arms.

the big bull, *Katmandoo,*
neck humped down, back legs kicked up
excited by five o'clock oat chop,
pushes his nose into the left bucket

his skull knob bruises into my forearm
pulls the pail from my fingers.

I run to the trough
and dump my remaining pail.

Pause. Breathe deep. Walk back.

Kick the big bastard under the jaw
with my red-toed rubber boot
scoop the pail from the mud,
leave him the chop, feed four more pails.

II.

Cow tongues scoop grain
off grey summerfallow dust,
noses buried between leaves of quack.
An inexperienced cousin stumbles
with a heavy pail, blunders
between two pawing cows
deciding who's boss.

The elder rushes past, sends him
spinning, nearly tripping over dry sod.
She buries her head into the other's ribs.
His fear and relief wash across each other.

His grin bathes his shallow confidence.
The smile cannot climb his cheeks
doesn't reach his eyes. His unsuredness
a hum rising from his slumped shoulders.

**Chaff**

I.

golden, dry autumn leaves
oat chaff smell swirls
from the tangled windrow

itchy inside grey sweat pants
down the collar of my shirt
baling straw on the open air tractor
the ground drive power-take-off

spins the straw into golden bales
rolling, the pickup throws straw
black belts roll yellow leaves
the colour of chaff in my nose

II.

night follows the edge of field
curls around sloughs, pockets
of trees curl out from fencelines

the truck follows the first round of swath,
straddles the windrow of threshed straw,
tousled hair standing behind the red combine

I relish the tidal play of my
gear shift thumb blister
as yellow leaves fall,
swirl against my striving

third gear bouncing over
every mole hill in the Cookie
Monster blue grain truck. Chaff
yellow leaves are caught
in the square headlight glare
and moonlight under disrobing trees

III.

a burnished yellow bale
slumps off tractor tines
drops a cloud of snow
falls with hesitation
crashes into snow
covered bedding
the half ton of straw rocks,
settles into cow nose hunger

I cut twines, pull them
through November rain ice
and resilient snow
a frozen outer layer fought free
gives cow tongues access

we muscle the bale over
onto its roundness
shoulder it across the corral rolling

spread gold
for pregnant cow comfort
autumn spread onto fresh snow

my shoulder against the bale
I smell again yellow
chaff in my nose

**Snow Steam Holes**

snow covers the swaths
gold cocooned in white rows
grain too wet to thresh and store

ancient open throat machine
spins wet gold bales which weigh twice the norm,
heat and stink like hog manure, bacterial

digestion, hot
in winter's cold grasp

feeding a race against spring's
warmth, potential fire

steam melts vent holes in snow.
The hay yard's winter sun
glares into near frozen eyes
of boys, men, sucked from Christmas dinner
by hungry cows, thirty below
fringes frost onto neglected whiskers

twine pulled with ease off fermented bales
too hot to touch heated grain.
Cows shove and bunt, horns hook into bellies
fight for their spot at unplanned silage

## In the Dead of Winter

in the dead of winter
calves come running
out of the uteri

Gelbveih cross
hybrid vigour
snorting fluid from nostrils

we haul them wet just born
plunked into the plastic sled
squirming and slippery behind the quad
the cow follows, licking into the barn

or better still
born inside
sucking buttery yellow
colostrum from pink teats

the dead of winter
has its accidental surprises
       frozen ears
       rubbed gently
       between warm hands.

       A shit nuts cow skull knob
       hooks into ribs. She's protecting
       the calf we're rescuing from the cold

dark smudges trekking the two hundred feet
from barn to house we slowly solidify
from between flakes, frozen ears prevented

three calves sheltered,
cows chased into stalls
reunited with the babies
we've carried off

a little weak one
still needs colostrum
it thaws in the microwave
while we cradle cups of tea

**Condensation Ice**

I flipped a round bale feeder
on the slope of the corral

it flipped an extra time
landing upside down
smacked a cow on the nose

she turned and there it was
a calf's feet hangin' out her back-side

three hours later after tea and supper he's born
and we load the black curly calf into the sled
pull him behind the ATV slowly
lure the cow through the purple barn door
into the last empty stall her nose leading her
sniffing she licks the calf

contained cow breath condenses, thickens ice
seals the door each day keeps calves warm
stretches the door latch beyond
the pressure of shoulder and hip. The ax
and my sweat hammers the ice away
shrapnel exploding in my face
the door latches tight

## Four Inches of Tongue

Dad spots the heifer,
a nose and four inches of tongue
protruding from her vagina,

*What the hell is she doing in calf!*

A question to be answered later

pushing the calf back in, he orders,

*Hold the cow boys,*
    *keep her off her side,*
        *he's got a leg back.*

He pulls the legs forward, one
then the other, hooks the chain
around the fetlocks
above the dew claws,
pulls, hisses,

    *Give me a hand!*

Teenage sons gather round,
get purchase on chains,
calf, surely dead, pops free
with a final sliding jerk, ribs still

*Get the slime outta them nostrils*

still not moving,
a pail of cold water
thrown on the calf
shocks a sharp breath,

*He's alive, breathing.*

*Get the heifer up,*
*        gotta get her up*
*                or she won't ever stand.*
*Push, pull boys.*

She heaves, we push
she's on her feet, unsteady
legs splayed wide, unsure
she licks the calf, begins
mothering, wobbly

the poor bastard's head
is swollen for a week
from her pelvic pressure.
We watch him suck,
keep an eye on him
'til he's running with the rest.

**At the Vet's**

I climb the box iron fence, walk the path
as the spring loaded head gate slams shut
around the cow's neck, against her shoulders.
I pass the squeeze cage holding her,
avoid the shit and blood stained cement,
spy a bovine probe, blue bullet shaped plastic
built to stimulate the prostate, semen sampling.

The vet pulls the calf with chains
and metal handles. The contractions
continue, she prolapses.
The calf bed hangs out of her,
looks like brains in a movie.
Washed, her uterus, this pink brain,
is pushed back in. Vagina locked
with plastic zip ties. A small space
left open for urine. Finished, the vet turns to us.

*Remember to remove them in three days.*

Another visit, the calf way too big.
The vet begins shaving the left side,
— on the right side her guts would fall out —
orange iodine, dish soap and a scrub brush
lather her hide until clean. Sterile?
He inserts the needle, attaches syringe,
pushes the plunger, local anesthetic
in four separate injections.
He draws the scalpel vertically
down through her thick hide.
Blood gathers, runs down her belly,
drips from her navel, pools,
meanders toward the floor drain.

Layers of skin and muscle hang open,
reveal the uterus. Calmly the vet says

>   *Oh this one's on the right horn,*[2]

Reaches all the way into the other side of her body,
pulls the calf from behind her bowels
into a large wheeled crate. curly forehead hair
wet and shiny, he gasps his first breaths.
A small white spot in the centre of his round skull,
a thin white strap above a front hoof.
His tongue slides into his nostril,
wanting to suck before he can stand
her tongue all over him roughly
mothering, getting his smell, his taste.

The vet stitches her uterus and muscles closed.
In her skin he leaves a small drainage hole
gaping fish mouthed low on her side.
She continues to lick her black bull calf.
Finished, the vet comments,

>   *He's a big one, must weigh one-twenty or better.*

---

2   the uterus has two horns.

*Liz*

Standing on a chair at the dining room window
I watch the truck pull down the drive

Old *Liz* in the back, corralled by cattle racks,
the metal and wood cage holds the black

and white cow I grew up petting,
watching the milk pail froth,
random streams shot into cat faces.

I whine,

>   *Mommy where is Liz going?*

*To market, she's old, wasn't in calf.*

The red truck pulls down the lane onto the highway.

I slowly climb off the dining room chair
Shuffle out the kitchen door
Down to the barn, gaze at *Billy, Liz's* last calf,
Chin resting on arms crossed along worn planks,
forehead pressed against rough wood.
The fence holds me there, hidden by tall grass.

# New Land

**The Versatile Eight Hundred**

Sun faded red. Burnt
with summer's glare
and diesel's compression.
Eight grey tires dust blown
turning blue under incoming clouds.

The door handle spins loosely
I climb in the window left open
my stomach barely clears
the mirror mount
as I feel with my toes
for a way into the seat
success with two small forearm scrapes
and a sore squeezed nipple.

I retrieve the blue water jug.

Hold in the Murphy switch
while the engine hesitates
and takes hold roaring.

Volunteer canola with green pods
clog the forty foot cultivator
behind the aging behemoth
the Versatile eight-hundred
with its slow hydraulics and duals bulging
a stone rolling between, marking rotations.

The grass, thistles, wild oats and canola
laid down in tangled piles of grey soil
all I leave standing are cat tails

exposed mice run for cover in slough grass
four crows and one fat fox feed

death in these fields continues
until rain clogs the eight-hundred's duals
with grey mud, slick and spinning
against shovels biting soil.

**Returning to the City**

the farm truck spitting
and sputtering
with my downshifting
revs roaring around the corner
then sputters for real
and finally I notice
the gauge on empty

hope against hope
and a leaky front tank,
I switch from the back

I walk to a neighbour's
Sunday morning on churchgoers' road
at the third house I find
a friendly dog and an open door

I phone home
leave a message
head cross country to summerfallow
on a sleep-in Sunday
start cultivating

the cultivator wing lifts
with the sharp ping
of a shovel wing breaking
against a stone too big
to slide between shanks

I don't lie on the grey lumps
changing shovels dirt in my hair
I'm returning to the city in a few hours

**Bush Pasture and an Old House**

A mile north of home,
on land newly bought
stands the Muir house. Walls lean
slowly slumping, roofless, floorless
surrounded by scrub willow
and second growth poplar
on stony land. Trees too thick for grass,
no feed, no paths, two hundred
and forty acre bush pasture

amber leaves flutter on white and black
poplars, the willowy slough edges.
Wind fallen trees, shattered and grey,
dead black poplars lie across
the grassed-over trail, amber ends jagged.
The single path crosses a slough, mud
solid with rock laid by a previous owner.
The red of undergrowth easily
mistaken for a half hidden cow

a lit match proclaims ownership
flames nearly singe the row of spruce

a house burnt, built with four-by-fours,
heavy six-inch nails, flanked
by newly mature spruce planted
before the roof fell in, to the north
rows and rows of purple irises
grew untended these thirty years.

After the fire the cellar's clay is blackened
with the ash of walls. A large grey stone
rests in the bottom, red flecked, fire cured,
stained with the black of heat.

Forty acres cleared and piled
land nearly reclaimed by finger
thick poplar, cheek by jowl, driving
only seeing four-year-old rows on each side
as they veer near. Trees laid down
and pushed tight torn roots pushed high.

In four-by-four, I drive
the old truck through the snow
search for wood densely packed on the windward side.

I apply used oil judiciously,
light with an aged *Western Producer.*
Snow melts in the rows' heat,
an orange haze rises over the January highway,
visible three miles away on our front porch.

Spring falls poplar seedlings
under the Roam plow discs and cultivator.

Roots picked by hand
build small pyres.
The last wood burnt

with forty-two acres open
in two hundred and forty
there's a chance we may find cows
in the wind escaping mosquitoes.

Gazing from the corner of the old yard
standing on the edge of the Muir house cellar
behind a now burnt wall, looking across
a mile of rolling pasture and field I see
grass in the place of trees
and above the glow of distant oats
a fringe of fenceline tree tops.

I love the random straight trees
rubbed red with cattle sweat, belly high.

In winter tall living lumber
proclaim life above snow
break the clean horizon

with white fanged hoar frost, crystal
spiderwebs on trembling branches are shaken
by the chainsaw's roar.

Above the tree's splintering crash
drifting on the wind, flakes of frost slide
down my neck. The yellow/white sawdust
shines bright on white snow.

The chainsaw buzzes off limbs.
Bucked into ten-foot lengths
trees become strong poplar planks
corrals to hide cows from the wind.

## New Land

two black trucks wind
through an army of forest
reconnoitering against a field
neglected thirty years

the trucks dance on the edge
weaving punch-drunk
through the overflow ruts
of too much slough

last year's brown leaves
float in June's puddles
lying in twin tracks
of the rarely traveled path
to a field with grid road access

leaves float over black tracks
crusting brown in the sun
diesel eyes puddle
in the rainbow ruts

between pothole sloughs
shaded by greedy willows
guarding the water

a shady place
a quiet cool lovely place
devoured by the D7 37A
growling
cracking trees
trapping rows
pushing fields clean

leaves a majestic new hilltop view

**Thirty-five Acres in Retrospect**

I.

Scanning my childhood's Big Pasture
from the high corner of thirty-five acres,
half the homestead's sixty-five,
its knolls are broken by strips of slough, moist
runnels pocked with damp black hoof holes.

The close cropped dusty carpet
broad to my childhood imagination
space enough to daydream and lose
a black dog over the hill. Today

on the stone pile
I stand and look
beyond barb wire
into old forbidden lands.

A pearl in the string of spring
runoff flowing out the fenced corner,
the pristine watery corner, bright green
stirred black by cows sinking belly deep
pulling their thousand pound bodies
onto the overgrown farm access
legs caked in black mud.
Free in the fresh May grasses,
timothy, broom, alfalfa.

*The History of Naming Cows*

II.

In the high corner of these thirty-five acres
standing on a rock, always in this spot

I feel a permanence in the pit of my stomach
watching geese flap in the slough
below the hollow's ditched run off.

I stand between stone piles in this hilltop
hollow, a bowl where two hilltops meet,
grey crusted after the spring melt.

Stones ripped from the ground by the tractor,
stone picker bats circling on their tracks
forcing rocks out of the ground,
dumping them in piles.

Willow bewhiskered stone record of sweat.

III.

This small pasture, the back thirty-five
short cropped grass worked down
frozen summer fallow grey
fractured by amber bladed sloughs
under late October clouds. Becomes

silver headed summer oats
the vista broken by rain killed slough grass,
new grass thrives under oat camouflage.

IV.

Walking back to the house,
I find the old stone picker
and remember riding the tractor's axle housing,
holding on to the fenders,
thinking the old ninety had great might
the stone picker teeth ripping rocks
from the ground.

Rusted iron basket filled
by four rocks speckled
with the ochre orange mould
of lichen growing on the white grace
of grey mottled stone.

The metal slats of the rock bucket
slowly sink into the grass.

Hints of red paint fading
white accents going ivory
one steel hydraulic line remains
bent and discarded, white on black dirt.

## Baling

The dead willow's grasping fingers
beckon, draw me forward toward
the humid mushroom patch I seek.

I expect no fungi from the weeks of heat.
Last year's dry slough grass, crisp,
crackles beneath my stride.
The crust of dried algae
spongy solid, water's last signature.

I walk on through the sun speckled forest
the silken leaves of wild roses, rough
edged, catch at my coarse blue jeans
as I emerge on the edge of the hay-
field's shorn dusty scalp.

**One Beer**

I nap the length of the field

sleep dreaming wild oats
I jerk awake
steering wheel in hand

wild oats between tires

fence in front
room to turn
I pull the steering wheel, hand over hand

behind the cultivator chews green slough

wheel held hard to the limit,
I flail at hydraulic levers

blundering on instinct

I hold the knob down,
lift shovels

I face from where I came
straighten wheel
   over-steer
      correct
         drop shovels down
bite earth

I breathe adrenaline, wide awake
I swear I will go to bed tonight

just one beer to cut the dust.

**The Baler**

after Uncle George's funeral
we drink half a case on the drive
to Englefeld dealing on a square baler
remembering our grandfather and his brother

we meet another dusty old man
buy his baler, hook up and pull away
what had held brand new pride

we drink the rest, pick up another
at Quill Lake, forty minutes up the road

towing a $500 baler
passing alongside a train
we honk the horn in response
to his crossroad blasts
raise our beers to the engineer
cheers us back a water bottle
picking up speed he blows his horn
as he passes us
his cruise set on Manitoba
ours set at fifty-five, barn
hay to be put up tomorrow.

**Salvaged**

I. June, 1988

Starting the Cat,
Bap Bap Bap —
the gasoline pup engine.
Bap Bap Bap —
subdued by the big engine's compression —
poot poot —
twin ether smoke rings rise leisurely,
diesel catches, growls unmuffled
by five inch straight pipe,
idles — roaring roughly

a newly purchased quarter,
pole barn full of horse shit
rat gnawed and time flattened.

Farm house, jagged teeth of glass
glare above the slowly collapsing cellar,
the vacant yard thistles armpit high,
the road, twin tracks through tall grass.

on the periphery old cars, rusting hulks
of a bygone barnyard mechanic.

The D7 crawler pares
topsoil from the slough edge,
turns, lifts that Cat's nose,
forces the blade down,
slides into brown clay, digs
a deep damp clay hole.

Pushes eight rusty cars in. Clay
cover raises the slough edge.
Topsoil spread. Sod lumps break
the wound's artificial arc.

Dad tosses into the truck box, frisbee like,
the salvaged Buick hubcap dog dish.


II. February 1989

The house's kitchen counters form basement bookshelves
for Dad's Louis L'Amours. Living room wood paneling

lines the new barn, blocks the wind
from newborn calves behind shiplap walls.

The garage is a granary whose corner of thistledown
reveals a mouse nest. Blind pink babies

squeal between smiling dog teeth.

III. June 1998

Teenage boys —
Peavey Mart plaid jackets, white
batting trailing from torn elbows —
jeans ripped on shingle nails,
we haul rafters, walls home. Raise
a granary, mouse tight, on uneven ground.

The house now half a skeleton,
garage torn off, rafters ripped off
the once ambitious expansion,
the ribbed studs of its walls exposed
to wind and rain. A carpet roll,
spineless, lies across rafters.

Gasoline douses an oatmeal grey mattress.
a poof of ignition. Dying flames
falter, catch carpets, build
a pink glow high as the ancient spruce.

IV. January 2007

The first homesteaders planted the roadside
spruce. Behemoths, they now tower, totter

in old age, ants chew at their hearts
as they shelter winter's grumpy bachelor bulls.

Woodpecker mined trunks, hollow hearted,
we fall dying trees, cut them into a pile of planks
a pool of shining white powder.

At Christmas Brett and I line
the purple barn built a generation ago
framed in spruce cut on Grandpa's permit.

Insulated and lined with dying spruce
from the dead homestead. We pound
nails into the second barn's birch
studs from the forest reserve, hardened
with twenty years of sun and heat.
Nails shoot across the barn. Muscle sore
we admire the fresh lumber's amber glow
in the old barn's dull light.

**Grandpa Stooking**

Ramrod straight in his sixties
white hair a thick fringe. The green
mesh Co-op hat matches the pants
of his fuel truck uniform.
Thin blue shirt, pale with washing,
rolled loosely above strong forearms.

Stooking hay behind the red baler,
he smiles at his small grandsons
snaps his false teeth out of his mouth
then sucks them back in.

Amazed we watch,
mesmerized by the sound.
The red baler writhes across the field.
The heavy weighted K-hunchunck.

Alfalfa flips on spinning tines, metal
arms and fingers force hay into cubes
square bales flip loose
jerk off the tailgate tied tight.

K-hunchunck childhood,
the roar of Dad's baling
and Grandpa's white-haired strength.

**Chainsaw Memories**

I'm home to help with fall branding
it's too miserable to handle cattle
the purple barn soaks in freezing mist
cold lies across cheek bones
seeps through wet gloves.

Instead we cut firewood
a forty-five-minute errand
I get bored loading behind
Brett's chainsaw speed

I wonder how we never kept up with Dad.

Then I remember the Cat's path
pushed into trees the way
a garden tiller chews ground

broken, fresh edged. The path
opened the way into firewood

three boys crammed the bench seat
knees clear of the gear shift
feet free of the four-by-four lever.

The truck bucking across fresh drifts
blown between shoulders of snow
the Cat blade path cuts
across the frozen quarter section
the way a snow shovel slides
across a shinny rink,

saw sputtering between his hands
the rewind whines. Without stress
he swings the two-stroke saw
until it roars blue exhaust.

He tromps into the snow
chases us back from the trees' path,
points to where we can play
in snow piles at the end of Cat tracks.
Ankles unsteady we climb the hard packed
piles, small trees pincushion out.

While Dad roars at trees, through firewood
we walk thin trunks slanted toward the sky
arms out, we fall into soft forest snow

until silence shouts

he's refueling the saw has half a load cut,
spread out across the sawdust stained snow

we start throwing wood
past him as he pours gas
and oil into the empty saw.

With chainsaw sore muscles
he heaves the last block
onto the heaping truck
way above our heads.

## A Christmas Story

Sitting around the oval hardwood table
we laugh at the things we got away with,
things Mom, Dad didn't know until too late.

I shot Shane in the foot
with the air rifle.
The pellet never broke the skin.

> *I meant to miss,*
> *splash him with mud*
> *like in a cowboy movie.*

The youngest brother turns to his fiancée.

> *We used to drive the tractor picking stones,*
> *me and Shane, together 'cause we were too small*
> *to clutch and shift all at once.*
>
> *Shane steered and clutched.*
> *He stood both feet on the clutch,*
> *holding onto the steering wheel,*
> *held the clutch in with his arms and legs.*
>
> *I'd shift, run the brakes and hydraulics.*
> *It was safe,* he grins. *He only ran me over once.*

Mom looks askance, he buries his face
in Krystal's hair, backtracks quickly.

> *Just my foot, it was fresh summer fallow,*
> *dirt loose, fluffy,*
> *didn't even hurt,*
> *much.*

Mom shakes her head
can't hide a half smile.

**The Need for Scotch**

The Sherman tank's army green thermos
holds my great uncle George's ashes.

Big around as an ice cream pail
but taller. Lid held in place
with green metal clamps

easy to open
like the lunch bucket it was

numbers pressed into its curved metal side
     8-5-1-3-3-7

placed in a purple velvet bag
the colour of a Crown Royal sack.

Dad paid him with a forty of whisky each fall
for his work on the farm alongside Grandpa.
Old bugger wouldn't accept money.

In the heat, George's wife, supported by two greying sons,
bends slowly, crumbles a bit of grey clay onto her loss.

Bundled against the cold, surrounded by trees,
above the secluded lake, shifting feet began
digging a hole for Grandpa. Cremated,
bundled in brown paper, wrapped
in pink baler twine he had saved
behind the seat of his truck for ten years.

No funeral, no obituary, only family
digging a grave late November, no frost
he would have loved discussing that fact

slowly lowering the brown paper package
trying to centre it, Grandma squared it
with the compass. The baler twine
fell into the hole, coiled on top of his ashes.

Handing Grandma the shovel for the first cover of clay
a classy move by my redneck brother.
Finally, lilies planted on top.
Dinner at my aunt's, I try
Scotch for the first time, an ode
to Grandpa. His drink in the army.
I love it.

**Reverie**

I baled windrows of dry alfalfa
curly leaf dust swirling behind.
With oily hands I steered up sidehills
around pothole sloughs and scattered
stone piles. I sat on the open air tractor
pulled the rock-o-matic, ground driven
bats spinning, throwing stone chips,
drive tire dragging a foot wide furrow

I return to where I calved cows.
Sleeplessly pulled calves, teats,
forced milk onto listless tongues,
a slow cup massaged down a wet throat.

I have been the matador to an angry mother,
made myself big, darted in front
of her matriarchal nose, while the calf
was tagged, treated and castrated.

I have nursed life into a set of lungs.
Bled life from them months later.

Knives, sharp, tractor idling,
Dad with the gun, me with the knife.
Legs folded beneath her body.
She lolled to her side kicking.
The jugular spurted
hot onto cropped grass.
Blood dried in my palm, browned the pasture dust.
Skinning her, she hung from the tines
hide dropped to the ground.

Dad grabbed her ears, jerked
and twisted her head loose.
I cut through jowls, excavated the grey tongue.
Finally, two halves of beef hung in cool night air.
We head in for tea and fresh liver, fried
in butter churned the night before.

# Acknowledgements

I would like acknowledge the support my parents, family and wife have given me in pursuit of my art.

I would also like to thank all the instructors who have influenced my work over the years. Especially worthy of note are Tim Lilburn, who pointed me in the direction of my voice and style, and Don Kerr without whose mentorship this book would not exist.

Some of these works have appeared previously in *The Antigonish Review, In Medias Res, The Sheaf* and the JackPine Press chapbook *Farm Raised*.

Finally, I would like to thank Hagios Press for its expertise in bringing this book to light.

Mitch Spray is a Saskatchewan poet with a background in farming, road construction, and academia. He grew up on a small mixed farm near Okla, Saskatchewan. Encouraged by his parents, he began pursuing writing seriously even before leaving home for university, where he obtained a Master of Arts in Aboriginal literature from the University of Saskatchewan.

In university Spray discovered poetry was the best fit for his episodic storytelling. His poetry has appeared in *The Antigonish Review* and in the chapbook *Farm Raised* (JackPine Press, 2011) which is bound in baler belting.

Mitch Spray has developed a variety of work skills. He can cut and saw lumber, calve, nurse and kill cattle, cut the meat and wrap it. He has changed a few toilets, wields a mean cleaver, and will clean the resulting dead chickens. He lives with his wife Hannah in Saskatoon where he works in agriculture sales.